Follow Me

L. LAWRENCE BRANDON, D.Min.

BK Royston Publishing
Jeffersonville IN
http://bkroystonpublishing.com
bkroystonpublishing@gmail.com

Cover and Layout: BK Royston Publishing

ISBN-13: 978-1-967282-95-1

Printed in the United States of America

Dedication

This project is wholeheartedly dedicated to my beloved momma, the late Mother Helen B. Lyons, and the late Dr. Oral Roberts, who have been the sources of inspiration, and who gave me strength when I thought of giving up. It is also dedicated to my wife, Wanda L. Brandon, my children, and my Praise Temple family who continually provided their moral, spiritual, emotional, and financial support. This project is also dedicated to Dr. James Barber, Ms. Celine Butler, and Mrs. Melanie Tollett who shared their words of advice and encouragement to finish this study.

Finally, I dedicate this work to the Almighty God, Jesus: thank you for the guidance, strength, power of mind, protection, and skills, as well as for giving me a healthy life. LORD, for this I rededicate my life to and for you.

Acknowledgements

Thanks also go to my wife, Wanda, and to the staff and members of Praise Temple of Shreveport, Louisiana, and of Evergreen Missionary Baptist Church of Oakland, California, for putting up with me sitting in the office for hours on end, and for providing guidance and a sounding board when required.

I particularly thank my children, Jasmine Nicole, Isaiah Jerel, Elijah Terel, and Queenesia Beatrice, for their patience and encouragement.

Thanks go to my eldest son, the late Larry Lawrence Brandon, III: I sorely miss you.

Table of Contents

Introduction

The most profound invitation ever extended to humanity came in two simple words: **"Follow Me."**

When Jesus Christ issued this command, He wasn't asking for seasonal admiration or casual agreement; He was calling for a complete redirection of life—a transformative journey known as Christian discipleship. This journey is not merely about believing certain facts; it is about actively becoming more like the One we follow.

But what does it truly look like to follow Him in a complex, modern world? How do we translate that ancient, beautiful call into the messy reality of our daily lives, our relationships, and our responsibilities?

This book, *Follow Me*, is your comprehensive guide to answering those questions. It is a roadmap designed to take you from a curious believer to a confident, reproducing disciple who knows their purpose and lives it out with joy and integrity.

The Journey Ahead

In the pages that follow, we will unpack the essential elements of discipleship, moving from foundation to faithful action.

The Foundation of the Calling We begin by establishing the necessary framework for this lifelong pursuit. **Understanding Discipleship** will define the core journey, followed by a deep dive into the vital necessity of **Prayer - Communicating with God**. We then explore the specific and personal nature of **The Call to Discipleship** that Jesus extends to each one of us.

Practicing the Life of Faith Once the foundation is set, we turn our attention to the habits that shape us. You will learn practical steps for **Growing in Faith**—how to nurture the inner life—and what it means to daily embody the Gospel through **Living Out Your Faith**. We emphasize that this journey is never meant to be traveled alone, exploring **The Importance of Community** and Christian fellowship.

The Mission and Multiplication A disciple is always on mission. We then look outward, detailing the fundamental principles of **Sharing the Gospel - Evangelism** and the immense privilege of **Discipling Others – Making Disciples**. This is the heart of Christ's commission: to multiply our lives through others.

Sustaining the Walk Finally, we address the realities of a committed life. You will gain tools for navigating the inevitable **Challenges in Discipleship** and learn how to honor God through

Stewardship - Managing God's Resources: Time, Talent and Treasure. Because we all stumble, we examine the life-altering power of **Forgiveness and Healing**.

We conclude with a powerful look at **The Rewards of Discipleship**—the eternal and temporal blessings that await those who choose to answer His call.

This is more than a book; it is an invitation. Wherever you are on your path—whether you are just starting to listen for His voice or you have been walking with Him for decades—this is your moment to lean in, learn, and live fully as a Christ-follower.

Are you ready to answer the call?

Let the journey begin.

Chapter 1:

Understanding Discipleship

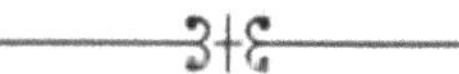

Scriptural Text:

And Jesus came and spake unto them, saying, All power is given unto me in heaven and in earth. Go ye therefore, and teach all nations, baptizing them in the name of the Father, and of the Son, and of the Holy Ghost: Teaching them to observe all things whatsoever I have commanded you: and, lo, I am with you always, even unto the end of the world. Amen.

Matthew 28:18-20 (KJV)

Learning Objectives:

1. Understand Discipleship as a Lifelong Journey of Faith, Growth, and Relationship

Learners will be able to articulate that discipleship is not a one-time achievement but a continuous process of spiritual development, personal transformation, and relational engagement with God and others.

2. Recognize the Role of Community and Fellowship in Spiritual Maturity

Learners will be able to explain how relationships within the Body of Christ—through mentorship, shared experiences, and small group fellowship—are essential for sustaining discipleship and advancing God's Kingdom.

3. Apply Principles of Support, Accountability, and Relational Care in Discipling Others

Learners will be able to identify practical ways to offer biblical guidance, emotional support, and spiritual encouragement to others, fostering growth and connection within diverse faith communities.

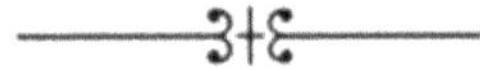

Definition of Discipleship

Discipleship: "Discipleship" is the process of "becoming more Christ-like," and is used "to describe *the process of spiritual growth*

Discipleship means helping someone grow in their faith and life. Like growing anything, a couple's relationships, a plant, a business, a ministry or a relationship with God, it's a journey. It doesn't happen overnight. You can't just get it with the blink of an eye or just by being hopeful or wishing or even just praying alone. It's the day by day, routines of life that helps you grow in your faith. It's the ups and down of life. It's the disappointments, hurt feelings, misunderstanding, the reconnections, the tears, pain and success that is all intertwined and a part of the discipleship journey. It's not a one-time destination. It's not a place and when you get there, you stand back, smile while patting yourself on your chest and say, 'I have arrived.' No ma'am and sir. Discipleship is daily, walking, working and growing until you die. Discipleship is learning about yourself, relying on your relationship with God and building a relationship with others on this earthly journey until we reach heaven and see our Master, Savior and King.

The Importance of Relationships

That's just the beginning and it has started with you alone. But the next part of the journey of discipleship is realizing that you as individual will learn to help others. The community has a whole must be willing and able to offer guidance and create a supportive community willing to share and connect throughout the Christian life and the discipleship journey.

In the Bible, discipleship emphasizes the importance of relationships. Now, I know that there are some modern sayings like, "we're in this thing together" or "we're in it to win it" to create a team, enthusiasm toward a goal or comradery. But discipleship requires relationships and we'll talk more later about fellowship. It's required. I realize that some people enjoy being alone, solitude and have an 'I don't need anybody attitude' but that's not God's plan. He created a family, a tribe, the Body of Christ, a Kingdom and His Kingdom is very relational. Establishing, sustaining, maintaining and growing relationship with Him, first and then the rest of the Body of Christ is key to the advancement of God's Kingdom and the detriment of the enemy's kingdom.

Safe Place to Grow

As people grow and experience life, they need a place to share their experience. The more experienced members of the faith should share practical, biblical advice to those that ask and need their Godly advice. This support, shoulder to cry on, Godly concern and advance should lead to positive outcomes, building up each other's faith and support the growth of others as they become disciples and develop on their discipleship journey. Always remember that discipleship is a journey and not a sprint.

Discipleship is an essential strategy for any ministry, crucial for church growth and personal spiritual development. People come from diverse backgrounds with various issues. They often face challenges that are hard to handle alone. Discipleship provides mentorship through teaching, experience, support, and accountability.

Global faith communities connect people, and discipleship builds strong bonds, allowing for personal sharing and fellowship. Global faith communities allow for connection across continents, traditions and culture differences but the cord that binds in their faith in the same God and His Word.

Modern Church and Small Groups

As the 21st-century church grows, it becomes a vibrant place for collaboration and inspiration. Ministry models have different structures, with small groups being the most common. These groups offer intimate settings to share ideas and solve real-life issues.

Small groups enhance congregational care by providing readily available resources and reducing neglect, unmet needs, and lack of accountability. They allow church members to engage and support each other, fostering communal faith growth.

Small groups connect various ministry approaches, engaging members at every level and strengthening local ministry. They provide a foundation for comprehensive congregational care, offering updated resources to improve members' lives. While small groups support discipleship, their primary goal is to offer fellowship and personal interaction opportunities.

Reflection

Chapter 2:

Prayer - Communicating with God

Scriptural Text:

"And it came to pass, that, as he was praying in a certain place, when he ceased, one of his disciples said unto him, Lord, teach us to pray, as John also taught his disciples. "Lord teach us to pray"

Luke 11:1 (KJV)

Learning Objectives:

1. Recognize Prayer as the Foundational Practice for Spiritual Growth and Intimacy with God

Learners will be able to explain how consistent, heartfelt prayer deepens the disciple's relationship with God, fosters communion, and sustains spiritual maturity throughout the discipleship journey.

2. Understand the Role of Prayer in Providing Guidance, Discernment, and Trust in God's Will

Learners will be able to describe how prayer invites the Holy Spirit's direction, cultivates trust in God's timing, and equips disciples to make faith-driven decisions in complex life situations.

3. Identify Prayer as a Source of Strength, Resilience, and Personal Transformation During Trials

Learners will be able to articulate how prayer empowers disciples to endure hardship, reframe challenges as growth opportunities, and experience inner renewal through communion with God.

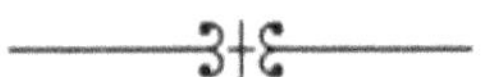

The Transformative Power of Prayer in Christian Discipleship

Discipleship is more than a spiritual journey; it is a covenant to follow Christ wholeheartedly, reflecting His teachings and embodying His love in every aspect of life. At the center of this journey lies a vital, often undervalued cornerstone: prayer. The practice of communicating with God is not merely a ritual—it is the lifeblood of Christian discipleship, a divine connection that empowers, guides, and transforms believers as they walk the challenging path of faith.

As the dawn of a new day broke over the small, hillside town, Emily sat quietly by her window, her Bible open before her. The soft rustling of leaves outside seemed almost to echo the stirrings of her heart, as she struggled with feelings of inadequacy in her discipleship journey. For Emily, the idea of following Christ had always carried a sense of awe and wonder. She had envisioned a life filled with bold acts of faith and selfless service. Yet, reality often felt far more ordinary, more difficult, and at times, even lonely. Doubts whispered to her, questioning her ability to truly embody the life of a disciple.

It was during this quiet moment that Emily turned to prayer—a practice she had learned from her grandmother but had not yet fully embraced. "God," she whispered softly, "I don't know if I'm doing enough. I want to follow You, but sometimes it feels so hard. Please, guide me and help me to understand what You want for my life."

This simple, heartfelt prayer marked a turning point in Emily's discipleship journey. Through consistent communication with God, she began to uncover the profound importance of prayer—not merely as an act of asking or receiving, but as the bridge to a deeper relationship with the One she sought to follow.

Prayer: The Foundation of Relationship

Prayer is not a monologue—it is a dialogue between the Creator and His beloved creation. For disciples, prayer serves as the foundation of their relationship with God, providing a sacred space to express joy, gratitude, struggles, and questions. Jesus Himself modeled this dependence on prayer throughout His earthly ministry. From the quiet wilderness to the crowded cities, He sought solitude to communicate with the Father, often rising early or retreating to remote places to pray.

In Luke 5:16, we read, “But Jesus often withdrew to lonely places and prayed.” This rhythm of withdrawing and connecting with God reflects the intimate bond that is at the heart of discipleship. Emily came to understand that her journey as a disciple was not about performing outward acts of faith alone—it was about abiding in Christ, remaining close to Him through prayer and trust.

As she continued to pray each morning, Emily began to notice subtle changes within herself. Her doubts began to quiet, replaced by a sense of peace that transcended her circumstances. The more she prayed, the more she recognized that God was not distant but present, listening to every word and guiding her steps.

Guidance and Discernment Through Prayer

One of the most important aspects of prayer in discipleship is its role in providing guidance and discernment. As disciples strive to align their lives with God's will, they often face decisions that require wisdom beyond human understanding. Through prayer, believers open their hearts to the Holy Spirit, inviting divine insight and clarity into their lives.

For Emily, prayer became the compass by which she navigated her discipleship journey. When she faced a difficult decision—whether to take on a demanding volunteer role at her church or focus on mentoring a struggling friend—she sought God's guidance in prayer. As she prayed, she felt led to choose the path that required deeper sacrifice, trusting that God's plan was far greater than her own. This experience taught her that prayer is not about receiving immediate answers; it is about cultivating trust in God's perfect timing and purpose.

In Proverbs 3:5-6, believers are encouraged to "Trust in the Lord with all your heart and lean not on your own understanding; in all your ways submit to Him, and He will make your paths straight." Emily found solace in these words, reminding herself that her role as a disciple was not to have all the answers but to faithfully seek God's direction through prayer.

Strength and Resilience in Trials

The journey of discipleship is fraught with challenges, trials, and moments of doubt.

Jesus warned His followers that the path would not be easy, stating in John 16:33, "In this world you will have trouble. But take heart! I have overcome the world." For disciples, prayer becomes the source of strength and resilience that equips them to endure difficulties with faith and hope.

Emily faced her own share of trials—a strained relationship with a coworker, financial struggles, and feelings of inadequacy in her ability to serve others effectively. At times, she felt overwhelmed, tempted to retreat from her calling as a disciple. Yet, in those moments, she turned to prayer, pouring out her fears and frustrations to God.

Through prayer, Emily discovered a profound truth: she was not alone. The presence of God comforted her, reminding her that He was her refuge and strength. In Psalm 46:1, the psalmist writes, "God is our refuge and strength, an ever-present help in trouble." These words became a lifeline for

Emily, inspiring her to persevere even when the path seemed impossible.

As she prayed, Emily also began to see her trials in a new light—not as obstacles but as opportunities to grow in faith and reliance on God. Through the refining fire of hardship, she became more compassionate, more patient, and more willing to surrender her plans to God's perfect will.

Communion and Transformation

Perhaps the most beautiful aspect of prayer in discipleship is its ability to transform hearts and minds. As disciples communicate with God, they are drawn into deeper communion with Him, experiencing His love, grace, and presence in ways that change their perspectives and priorities.

Emily's prayers gradually shifted from requests to praises. She began to see her relationship with God not as a means to an end but as the ultimate treasure of her life. Her heart was softened, her faith strengthened, and her desire to serve others deepened. Prayer became not only a practice but a lifestyle—a constant connection to the One who called her to discipleship.

In Romans 12:2, Paul urges believers to "be transformed by the renewing of your mind." Prayer serves as the catalyst for this renewal, allowing disciples to exchange their fears for faith, their doubts for trust, and their self-centered desires for God-centered purpose.

Conclusion

Christian discipleship is a journey marked by sacrifice, commitment, and transformation. At the heart of this journey lies prayer—a powerful practice that connects believers to God, offering guidance, strength, and communion. For Emily, the importance of prayer became evident as she navigated the challenges and joys of following Christ. It was through prayer that she discovered the peace of abiding in God's presence, the wisdom to make difficult decisions, and the resilience to endure trials.

Ultimately, prayer is not just an act but a relationship—a sacred dialogue that invites disciples into the fullness of life in Christ. As believers embrace the transformative power of prayer, they are equipped to reflect God's glory, grow in faith, and experience the richness of His presence. For every disciple, the journey of following Christ is illuminated and sustained by the beautiful practice of prayer.

Reflection

Chapter 3:

The Call to Discipleship

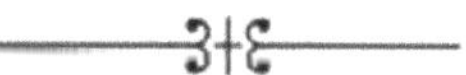

Scriptural Text:

For which of you, intending to build a tower, sitteth not down first, and counteth the cost, whether he have sufficient to finish it? Lest haply, after he hath laid the foundation, and is not able to finish it, all that behold it begin to mock him, Saying, This man began to build, and was not able to finish.

Luke 14:28-30 (KJV)

And he saith unto them, Follow me, and I will make you fishers of men.

Matthew 4:19 (KJV)

Learning Objectives:

1. Understand the Transformative Nature of Christian Discipleship

Learners will be able to explain how discipleship involves a lifelong commitment to follow Jesus, embody His teachings, and surrender personal desires in pursuit of spiritual growth and intimacy with God.

2. Recognize the Role of Sacrifice and Obedience in the Discipleship Journey

Learners will be able to identify key areas where disciples are called to sacrifice—such as time, comfort, and worldly attachments—and describe how obedience to God's will reflects true devotion to Christ.

3. Evaluate the Cost and Rewards of Discipleship Through Biblical and Personal Examples

Learners will be able to assess the challenges disciples may face, including persecution and trials, and articulate how enduring these costs leads to spiritual maturity, deeper faith, and eternal reward, using examples like the Apostle Paul.

Christian discipleship is a profound journey that calls believers to follow Jesus Christ wholeheartedly, embody His teachings, and surrender their lives to His will. At its core, discipleship is not merely an affiliation or a title—it is a transformative commitment that requires sacrifice, unwavering devotion, and an understanding of the cost associated with being a follower of Christ. This journey is not for the faint of heart; it challenges individuals to live counter-culturally, deny themselves, and prioritize God above all else.

Sacrifice

The idea of sacrifice is deeply ingrained in Christian discipleship. Jesus Himself set the ultimate example of sacrifice through His life, ministry, and death on the cross. He willingly gave up His heavenly glory to dwell among humanity, taking on the form of a servant and laying down His life for the salvation of the world. In Philippians 2:6-8, Paul describes how Jesus "humbled himself by becoming obedient to death—even death on a cross." This selfless act of love serves as the foundation for Christian discipleship and sets the standard for what it means to follow Christ.

For disciples, sacrifice begins with a willingness to let go of personal ambitions, desires, and comforts in order to align one's life with God's will. In Luke 9:23, Jesus states, "Whoever wants to be my disciple must deny themselves and take up their cross daily and follow me." This powerful statement emphasizes that discipleship is not a casual endeavor; it requires a deliberate choice to put God first, even when it comes at a cost. Whether it involves sacrificing time, resources, or personal preferences, discipleship demands a heart that is fully surrendered to God.

One significant area of sacrifice in discipleship is the renunciation of worldly attachments. Jesus often spoke about the dangers of placing trust in material wealth and earthly possessions. In Matthew 6:19-

21, He advises His followers to "store up for yourselves treasures in heaven" rather than clinging to temporal riches. For many disciples, this may mean re-evaluating priorities, simplifying lifestyles, and using resources to serve others and advance God's kingdom. While this can be challenging, it is a reminder that true fulfillment is found in Christ, not in the fleeting pleasures of the world.

Commitment

Commitment is another cornerstone of Christian discipleship. To be a disciple is to be wholly devoted to Christ, not just in moments of convenience but in every aspect of life. This commitment requires a steadfast determination to follow Jesus, even in the face of adversity, doubt, or opposition. In John 15:5, Jesus compares His followers to branches connected to a vine, illustrating the importance of abiding in Him to bear fruit. This abiding relationship underscores that discipleship is not a one-time decision but a lifelong journey of faith and growth.

Commitment to discipleship also involves obedience to God's commands. Jesus said in John 14:15, "If you love me, keep my commands." Obedience is not about legalism or fear but about a genuine desire to honor God and live according to His Word. This commitment often involves making difficult choices, such as standing firm in faith when faced with temptation or upholding biblical principles in a culture that may reject them. It is a commitment to live with integrity, humility, and compassion, reflecting the character of Christ in all things.

The Cost of Discipleship

The cost of discipleship is perhaps one of the most challenging aspects of following Jesus. Jesus did not shy away from addressing the realities of what it means to be His disciple. In Luke 14:25-33, He speaks about the need to count the cost, likening discipleship to a builder calculating expenses before constructing a tower. He warns that those who follow Him must be prepared to forsake everything, including family, possessions, and even their own lives, if necessary.

For some, the cost of discipleship involves persecution or rejection. Jesus warned His disciples that the world would hate them because of their allegiance to Him (John 15:18-20). This reality continues today, as many believers face hostility, discrimination, or even physical harm for their faith. The cost of discipleship also includes enduring trials and challenges that test one's faith and resolve. However, these difficulties are not without purpose; they refine character, deepen reliance on God, and bring glory to His name.

Despite the sacrifices, commitment, and cost, the rewards of discipleship far outweigh the challenges. Jesus promises His followers that those who lose their lives for

His sake will find true life (Matthew 16:25). This paradox illustrates that surrendering to God's will leads to freedom, joy, and fulfillment. Discipleship opens the door to an intimate relationship with God, the privilege of participating in His redemptive work, and the hope of eternal life.

The Apostle Paul is a powerful example of someone who embraced the cost of discipleship with unwavering faith. Once a persecutor of Christians, Paul encountered Jesus on the road to Damascus and was forever transformed. He gave up his status, possessions, and comfort to preach the gospel, enduring imprisonment, beatings, and hardship along the way. In Philippians 3:7-8, Paul writes, "But whatever were gains to me I now consider loss for the sake of Christ." His life testifies to the profound impact of living fully committed to Christ, regardless of the cost.

Ultimately, Christian discipleship is a journey that mirrors the life of Jesus—a life marked by love, humility, and selflessness. It is a call to leave behind the familiar and step into a deeper relationship with God, trusting Him to lead and provide. While the path may be challenging, it is also deeply rewarding, offering believers the opportunity to grow in faith, reflect God's glory, and experience the richness of His presence.

Conclusion

In conclusion, Christian discipleship involves sacrifice, commitment, and a willingness to embrace the cost of following Jesus. It is a journey that challenges believers to let go of their own desires, remain steadfast in their faith, and prioritize God above all else. While the demands of discipleship may be great, the rewards are immeasurable—a life transformed by grace, a heart aligned with God's will, and the promise of eternal fellowship with Him. As disciples navigate the ups and downs of this journey, they can find strength and encouragement in the example of Christ, who demonstrated the ultimate act of love and sacrifice for the sake of humanity. In every step of discipleship, God's presence and faithfulness serve as a constant reminder that the cost is worth it, and the journey leads to abundant life in Him.

Reflection

Reflection

Chapter 4:

Growing in Faith

Scriptural Text:

For as many as are led by the Spirit of God, they are the sons of God.

Romans 8:14 (KJV)

Howbeit when he, the Spirit of truth, is come, he will guide you into all truth: for he shall not speak of himself; but whatsoever he shall hear, that shall he speak: and he will shew you things to come. John 16:13 (KJV)

Learning Objectives:

1. Understand the Role of the Holy Spirit in Transforming Routine Discipleship into a Vibrant Relationship with God

Learners will be able to explain how Spirit-led discipleship moves beyond religious routines to cultivate intimacy, guidance, and transformation through communion with the Holy Spirit.

2. Recognize the Holy Spirit as Teacher, Guide, and Source of Empowerment in the Discipleship Journey

Learners will be able to describe how the Holy Spirit illuminates Scripture, provides discernment in decision-making, and empowers believers to respond with Christlike character in challenging circumstances.

3. Appreciate the Communal Nature of Spirit-Led Discipleship and Its Impact on Christian Growth

Learners will be able to identify how the Holy Spirit fosters unity, mutual support, and shared purpose within the Body of Christ, emphasizing that discipleship is a relational journey, not a solitary pursuit.

Walking with the Spirit: A Journey of Christian Discipleship

The rain pattered softly against the window as Sarah closed her Bible. Another morning devotion completed, yet something felt missing. For years, her Christian walk had felt like following a checklist: church on Sundays, Bible reading in the mornings, prayer before meals, and occasional volunteer work. She was doing everything right—at least according to the discipleship book her small group was studying—but the vibrant relationship with God that others spoke about seemed just beyond her reach.

"Lord," she whispered, "I'm following all the rules, but where's the life in this journey?"

Sarah's experience reflects a common struggle in Christian discipleship. Many believers diligently follow spiritual disciplines and practices, yet find themselves wondering if there's more to following Christ than merely adhering to religious routines. What's often missing in this equation is the animating presence of the Holy Spirit—the divine guide Jesus promised would lead us into all truth.

The Missing Piece

Christian discipleship, at its core, is not merely about following a set of practices but about following a Person. Jesus's invitation was simple yet profound: "Follow me." The early disciples didn't have discipleship manuals or twelve-week programs. They had a relationship with the living Christ, and after His ascension, the promised Holy Spirit who would continue His work in them.

The Apostle Paul understood this when he wrote to the Galatians: "Since we live by the Spirit, let us keep in step with the Spirit" (Galatians 5:25). This imagery of "keeping in step" portrays discipleship not as a solo performance but as a divine dance with the Spirit leading.

For Sarah, this realization came gradually. One evening during a church worship service, she found herself overwhelmed by a sense of God's presence. Instead of rushing through her usual prayer list, she simply sat in silence, aware of something—Someone—stirring within her heart.

"I felt like I was finally connecting with God rather than just talking at Him," she later told her friend Michael. "It was like the difference between reading a letter from someone and sitting across the table from them."

The Spirit as Teacher

Jesus promised His disciples that the Holy Spirit would "teach you all things and will remind you of everything I have said to you" (John 14:26). Christian discipleship involves learning, but with an extraordinary Teacher who brings Scripture alive and makes it personally relevant.

Michael had experienced this firsthand. As a theology student, he had access to countless commentaries and scholarly resources, but his most profound insights came during moments of quiet reflection.

"Sometimes I'll read a passage I've studied academically dozens of times," he explained to Sarah, "but then the Spirit highlights it in a completely new way that speaks directly to my current situation. No commentary could do that."

This dynamic teaching relationship distinguishes Christian discipleship from mere religious education. The Spirit doesn't simply impart information; He transforms hearts and minds through divine illumination.

"When the Spirit of truth comes, he will guide you into all the truth," Jesus promised (John 16:13). This guidance goes beyond intellectual understanding to wisdom for daily living—wisdom that often defies conventional logic but aligns perfectly with God's purposes.

The Power for Transformation

Three months after her moment of clarity, Sarah found herself facing a family crisis. Her brother had relapsed into addiction, and old patterns of anger and resentment threatened to overwhelm her. In previous years, she would have relied on willpower and Christian principles to manage these emotions.

This time was different.

"I felt completely incapable of responding with love," she recalled. "But I remembered something our pastor had said about the fruit of the Spirit not being something we produce through effort but something the Spirit produces through us when we remain connected to Him."

Instead of striving to manufacture forgiveness, Sarah acknowledged her inability and invited the Holy Spirit to work through her weakness. Gradually, a compassion beyond her natural capacity began to flow. The situation hadn't changed, but she had—or rather, the Spirit had changed her from within.

This exemplifies another crucial aspect of Spirit-led discipleship: transformation happens not through human effort but divine empowerment. Paul emphasizes this in Romans 8:13 when he writes about putting to death the misdeeds of the body "by the Spirit." The Christian life isn't about trying harder but about yielding more completely to the Spirit's work.

Guided by the Spirit

Six months into her renewed spiritual journey, Sarah faced a major career decision. Two job offers lay before her—one offering financial security and professional advancement, the other aligned with her sense of calling but fraught with uncertainty.

"How do I know which path God wants me to take?" she asked Michael during their weekly coffee meeting.

"The Spirit often guides through a sanctified wisdom," Michael suggested. "It's not always about dramatic signs or voices. Sometimes it's about learning to recognize His gentle nudges, the inner witness that grows stronger as you walk with Him."

This guidance comes in various forms: through Scripture illuminated by the Spirit, through the counsel of Spirit-filled believers, through circumstances, and through that still, small voice within. Learning to discern this guidance is a critical discipline in Christian discipleship.

For Sarah, clarity came through a combination of prayer, counsel, and an inexplicable peace about the less secure option. "It doesn't make sense on paper," she admitted, "but I have this deep conviction that this is where God is leading me."

Community in the Spirit

One year after her spiritual awakening, Sarah found herself leading a small discipleship group. The irony wasn't lost on her—the woman who had once felt spiritually stagnant was now helping others navigate their own journeys.

"The most important thing I've learned," she told her group during their first meeting, "is that discipleship isn't a solo expedition. We need each other, and we all need the Spirit."

This communal aspect of Spirit-led discipleship echoes throughout Scripture. The early church in Acts was marked by a powerful sense of unity and shared purpose, all facilitated by the Holy Spirit. Paul's discussion of spiritual gifts in 1 Corinthians emphasizes that these diverse manifestations of the Spirit are given "for the common good" (1 Corinthians 12:7).

Michael, now a pastor, often reminded his congregation: "The Holy Spirit rarely leads us into isolation. Even when He led Jesus into the wilderness, it was for a season and purpose. The Spirit typically leads us into deeper community, not away from it."

The Ongoing Journey

Three years after that rainy morning when she had questioned her spiritual journey, Sarah sat in the same chair with her Bible open. The disciplines hadn't changed—she still read Scripture, prayed, attended church, and served others. But everything was different.

"It's like I was once looking at a map of the Christian life," she reflected, "but now I'm actually walking the terrain with the best Guide possible."

The disciplines had become not obligations but opportunities for communion with the Spirit. Scripture had transformed from a rulebook to a love letter, illuminated by its divine Author. Prayer had evolved from monologue to dialogue, with periods of listening becoming as important as speaking.

This is the essence of Spirit-led discipleship—not a program to complete but a relationship to nurture, not rules to follow but a Person to follow, not a destination to reach but a journey to embrace.

As Paul writes in 2 Corinthians 3:18, "And we all, who with unveiled faces contemplate the Lord's glory, are being transformed into his image with ever-increasing glory, which comes from the Lord, who is the Spirit."

The Spirit who hovered over the waters at creation now hovers over our lives, bringing order from chaos, light from darkness, and new life from what was dormant. In Christian discipleship, He is not merely a helper along the way but the very breath that sustains the journey.

Reflection

Reflection

Chapter 5:

Living Out Your Faith

Scriptural Text

"Ye are the light of the world. A city that is set on
an hill cannot be hid. 15 Neither do men light a
candle, and put it under a bushel, but on a
candlestick; and it giveth light unto all that are in
the house. 16 Let your light so shine before men,
that they may see your good works, and glorify
your Father which is in heaven."

Matthew 5:14-16 (KJV)

Learning Objectives:

1. Identify Key Challenges in the Discipleship Journey and Their Spiritual Significance

Learners will be able to recognize and articulate common obstacles in Christian discipleship—such as self-denial, temptation, suffering, compromise, and spiritual apathy—and explain how these challenges serve as opportunities for growth, perseverance, and deeper reliance on God.

2. Understand the Role of Obedience, Humility, and Surrender in Spiritual Transformation

Learners will be able to describe how the disciplines of obedience, humility, and surrender to God's will contribute to the lifelong process of becoming more like Christ and experiencing spiritual maturity.

3. Explore the Importance of Community, Scripture, and the Holy Spirit in Sustaining Discipleship

Learners will be able to explain how fellowship with other believers, engagement with God's Word, and dependence on the Holy Spirit provide strength, guidance, and encouragement throughout the discipleship journey.

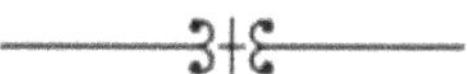

Christian discipleship is a lifelong journey of following Jesus Christ, emulating His teachings, and committing oneself to the transformative process of becoming more like Him. At its heart, discipleship calls for obedience, humility, and a willingness to surrender to God's will. However, this journey is not without its challenges or temptations. The path of discipleship often brings trials that test faith, perseverance, and commitment, but these moments of struggle also offer opportunities for growth, deeper reliance on God, and spiritual maturity.

Deny Yourself

One of the first challenges in Christian discipleship is the call to deny oneself and take up the cross daily, as instructed by

Jesus in Luke 9:23. This requires a deliberate choice to prioritize God's will above personal desires, ambitions, or comforts. In a culture that frequently promotes self-gratification and individualism, denying oneself can feel counterintuitive and challenging. Whether it is the temptation to pursue worldly success at the expense of spiritual values or the struggle to let go of harmful habits, the act of self-denial demands discipline and a deep trust in God's purposes.

Temptation

Another significant challenge is the battle against temptation. Jesus Himself faced temptation during His time on earth, as seen in His encounter with Satan in the wilderness (Matthew 4:1-11). This narrative highlights the reality that even the most devoted followers of God are not immune to temptation. For modern disciples, these temptations may take many forms—materialism, pride, envy, or unhealthy relationships. The enemy often seeks to distract believers from their purpose, offering fleeting pleasures or false security in exchange for their devotion. Overcoming temptation requires steadfast reliance on God's Word, prayer, and the power of the Holy Spirit.

Suffering

Discipleship also involves enduring trials and hardships. Following Christ does not guarantee a life free from suffering; in fact, Jesus warned His disciples that they would face persecution and difficulties for His name's sake (John 16:33). For many believers, this challenge manifests as ridicule, isolation, or discrimination for standing firm in their faith. In some parts of the world, discipleship even comes with the risk of physical harm or imprisonment. These hardships test the resolve of believers, pushing them to deepen their faith and trust in God's sovereignty. James 1:2-4 reminds us that trials produce perseverance and maturity, transforming challenges into opportunities for spiritual growth.

Compromise

One of the subtler yet pervasive challenges of discipleship is the temptation to compromise. In an age where moral relativism and cultural pressures are prevalent, it can be difficult to remain unwavering in biblical principles. Whether it is the pressure to conform to societal norms or the desire to avoid conflict, disciples may be tempted to dilute their convictions to fit in or gain acceptance. However, Jesus calls His followers to be the "salt of the earth" and the "light of the world" (Matthew 5:13-16), emphasizing the importance of standing out and living as a testament to God's truth.

Spiritual Apathy

The challenge of spiritual apathy is another obstacle on the path of discipleship. Over time, the initial zeal and enthusiasm for following Christ can wane, leading to complacency in prayer, worship, and studying God's Word. This spiritual dryness can make it difficult to maintain a vibrant and intimate relationship with God. Disciples may find themselves going through the motions without experiencing true transformation or joy. To combat this, it is essential to intentionally rekindle one's passion for God through regular devotion, fellowship with other believers, and seeking the guidance of the Holy Spirit.

Additionally, Christian discipleship often involves navigating the complexities of relationships. Disciples are called to love others, forgive those who wrong them, and serve selflessly, even when it is difficult. This can be particularly challenging in the face of conflict, betrayal, or strained relationships. The call to love one's enemies and pray for those who persecute them (Matthew 5:44) is a profound yet challenging aspect of discipleship. It requires humility, grace, and a heart aligned with God's love.

Balancing the demands of discipleship with the responsibilities of daily life is yet another challenge. Work, family, and other commitments can sometimes feel overwhelming, leaving little room for intentional spiritual growth. The busyness of life can distract disciples from their calling, leading to a sense of disconnection from God. Finding a healthy balance requires prioritizing time with God and seeking His guidance in managing responsibilities.

Despite these challenges, Christian discipleship is a journey filled with hope and promise. While the path may be difficult, it is also one of profound transformation and joy. Disciples are not alone in their journey; they are empowered by the Holy Spirit, sustained by God's Word, and supported by the fellowship of other believers. The challenges of discipleship, though daunting, serve as opportunities to draw closer to God, deepen faith, and reflect His character.

In the face of temptation, disciples can find strength in Jesus' example and in the promises of Scripture. James 4:7 encourages believers to resist the devil, assuring them that he will flee. Through prayer and reliance on the Holy Spirit, disciples can overcome the distractions and enticements of the world. When trials arise, the assurance of God's presence and faithfulness offers comfort and hope. Romans 8:28 reminds believers that God works all things together for the good of those who love Him, even in the midst of suffering.

The journey of discipleship is also marked by growth in community. Fellowship with other believers provides encouragement, accountability, and support, helping disciples navigate challenges together. Sharing one another's burdens and celebrating victories fosters a sense of unity and strengthens faith. Ecclesiastes 4:9-10 emphasizes the value of companionship, stating that two are better than one because they can lift each other up in times of need.

Above all, discipleship is about abiding in Christ and finding strength in Him. Jesus reminds His followers in John 15:5 that apart from Him, they can do nothing. By staying connected to Him through prayer, worship, and Scripture, disciples can face challenges with confidence and resilience. The journey of discipleship may be demanding, but it is also deeply rewarding. It is a path that leads to a closer relationship with God, a life of purpose, and the hope of eternal fellowship with Him.

Conclusion

In conclusion, Christian discipleship is a journey that requires perseverance, commitment, and trust in God. The challenges and temptations faced along the way are not obstacles to be feared but opportunities for growth and transformation. Through God's grace, the support of fellow believers, and reliance on His Word, disciples can overcome these difficulties and continue to walk faithfully with Christ. The journey may be demanding, but it is a path worth pursuing, one that leads to a deeper understanding of God's love and a life that glorifies Him. In every challenge, discipleship reminds believers that they are not alone—God walks with them, guiding and strengthening them every step of the way.

Reflection

Chapter 6:

The Importance of Community

Scriptural Text:

For where two or three are gathered together in my name, there am I in the midst of them.

Matthew 18:20 (KJV)

Learning Objectives:

1. Understand the Role of Fellowship in Sustaining and Enriching the Discipleship Journey

Learners will be able to explain how fellowship provides strength, encouragement, and spiritual enrichment, helping believers persevere through trials and grow in faith within a supportive community.

2. Recognize Fellowship as a Reflection of God's Nature and a Catalyst for Spiritual Transformation

Learners will be able to describe how fellowship mirrors the unity of the Trinity, nurtures the fruits of the Spirit, and fosters Christlike character through shared worship, study, and service.

3. Explore the Functions of Accountability, Evangelism, and Collective Learning Within Christian Community

Learners will be able to identify how fellowship promotes mutual accountability, equips believers to serve and share the gospel, and deepens understanding of Scripture through communal engagement.

Christian discipleship is more than a personal commitment; it is a transformative journey that calls believers to follow the teachings of Jesus Christ and emulate His life. Discipleship is a continuous process, shaping individuals into mature Christians who reflect Christ's love, character, and mission. However, this spiritual growth does not occur in isolation—it is nurtured and sustained through fellowship. Fellowship, the unity and community of believers, plays a vital role in discipleship by providing support, encouragement, accountability, and opportunities for spiritual enrichment.

Fellowship

The importance of fellowship is evident in the early church's practices, as described in Acts 2:42-47. These verses paint a picture of believers who gathered regularly to learn from the apostles, pray together, share meals, and support one another. They exhibited generosity and unity, and their shared faith not only strengthened their community but also served as a testimony to others. The early church understood the significance of fellowship in fostering spiritual growth and sustaining the faith of individuals. This communal aspect of discipleship remains relevant today, as believers face challenges and distractions that can hinder their spiritual journey.

Fellowship is not merely social interaction; it is a spiritual connection that unites believers as members of the body of Christ. The Apostle Paul emphasizes this interconnectedness in 1 Corinthians 12:12-27, using the metaphor of a body with many parts. Each believer plays a unique role in the body, and no part can function effectively in isolation. This analogy underscores the need for fellowship in discipleship. Just as a body thrives when its parts work together, Christians grow spiritually when they engage in meaningful relationships with others. Fellowship reminds believers that they are part of a larger, divinely orchestrated community.

Strength in Fellowship

Through fellowship, believers find strength and encouragement to persevere in their discipleship journey. Life is often filled with trials, temptations, and uncertainties that can test one's faith. In such moments, the support of a Christian community becomes invaluable. Encouragement from fellow believers uplifts the weary, strengthens the doubting, and restores hope to the disheartened. The writer of Hebrews captures this idea in Hebrews 10:24-25, urging believers to "consider how we may spur one another on toward love and good deeds" and to "not give up meeting together." Fellowship provides a space where individuals can share their burdens and joys, knowing they are surrounded by others who care and are willing to walk alongside them.

Accountability in Fellowship

Another key aspect of fellowship in discipleship is accountability. Accountability ensures that believers remain faithful to their commitment to Christ and live in accordance with His teachings. Proverbs 27:17 illustrates this concept: "As iron sharpens iron, so one person sharpens another." Within a community, individuals are challenged to grow, confront their shortcomings, and pursue righteousness. Accountability in fellowship fosters honesty, humility, and mutual encouragement, creating an environment where spiritual growth is both supported and expected. This accountability is not about judgment but about loving guidance and mutual responsibility.

God's Word and Truths in Fellowship

Furthermore, fellowship deepens believers' understanding of God's Word and His truths. In a community setting, Christians have opportunities to study the Bible together, discuss its teachings, and apply its principles to their lives. Group learning allows individuals to benefit from diverse perspectives, enhancing their comprehension and appreciation of Scripture. Fellowship also includes collective worship, where believers come together to praise and glorify God. This shared experience of worship fosters unity and reinforces the communal aspect of discipleship. Through fellowship, believers grow not only in their knowledge of God's Word but also in their relationship with Him.

The role of fellowship extends beyond the boundaries of the church. It equips believers to serve others and to share the gospel. In fellowship, Christians develop a sense of compassion and responsibility toward their community and the world. Fellowship inspires acts of service, whether through mentoring, volunteering, or supporting those in need. It encourages believers to live out their faith in practical ways, demonstrating Christ's love and kindness. Additionally, fellowship provides a platform for evangelism, as the unity and love within a Christian community serve as a powerful testimony to others. Jesus Himself emphasized this in John 13:35, saying, "By this everyone will know that you are my disciples, if you love one another."

God's Nature in Fellowship

Fellowship also reflects the nature of God, who exists in perfect relationship as Father, Son, and Holy Spirit. The triune God models unity, love, and harmony, qualities that believers are called to embody in their relationships. Engaging in fellowship allows Christians to mirror this divine relationship, strengthening their bond with one another and their connection to God. This communal aspect of discipleship is not only a blessing for believers but also a reflection of God's character and a testimony to the transformative power of His love.

Address Challenges in Fellowship

Moreover, fellowship addresses the challenges and distractions that can arise in discipleship. In a world filled with competing priorities, fellowship helps believers remain focused on their spiritual growth and their commitment to Christ. It provides a safe and supportive environment where individuals can share their struggles and receive guidance. Fellowship combats isolation and loneliness, reminding believers that they are part of a community that cares for them and supports their journey. It reinforces the truth that discipleship is not a solitary endeavor but a shared experience.

Spiritual Enrichment in Fellowship

Fellowship also fosters spiritual enrichment, encouraging believers to cultivate the fruits of the Spirit, as described in Galatians 5:22-23. Love, joy, peace, patience, kindness, goodness, faithfulness, gentleness, and self-control are not only virtues but also harmonics that align believers with God's will. Through fellowship, these qualities are nurtured and expressed, transforming individuals and communities alike. Fellowship becomes a space where believers are inspired to grow in their faith and to reflect Christ's character in their interactions with others.

In conclusion, Christian discipleship is a journey that is both personal and communal. It is enriched and sustained by fellowship, which provides strength, encouragement, accountability, and opportunities for spiritual growth. Fellowship reminds believers that they are part of a larger community, united in their faith and their commitment to Christ. It deepens their understanding of God's Word, equips them to serve others, and reflects the nature of God. As believers engage in fellowship, they experience the fullness of life in Christ, growing together in faith and becoming living testimonies of His love. Through fellowship, discipleship becomes not only a path to spiritual maturity but also a reflection of God's divine plan for His people—a plan that calls them to walk together in unity, love, and purpose.

Reflection

Chapter 7:

Sharing the Gospel - Evangelism

Scriptural Text:

And Jesus came and spake unto them, saying, All
power is given unto me in heaven and in earth. 19
Go ye therefore, and teach all nations, baptizing
them in the name of the Father, and of the Son,
and of the Holy Ghost: 20 Teaching them to
observe all things whatsoever I have commanded
you: and, lo, I am with you always, even unto the
end of the world. Amen.

Matthew 28:18-20 (KJV)

Ye are the salt of the earth: but if the salt have lost his savour, wherewith shall it be salted? it is thenceforth good for nothing, but to be cast out, and to be trodden under foot of men.

Matthew 5:13 (KJV)

Learning Objectives:

1. Understand the Biblical Call to Be Salt and Light in Everyday Life

Learners will be able to explain how Jesus's teachings in Matthew 5 call believers to live visibly and intentionally, allowing their faith to influence relationships, conversations, and environments beyond the church walls.

2. Recognize Evangelism as an Essential Expression of Christian Discipleship

Learners will be able to describe how sharing one's faith—through simple acts of invitation, conversation, and authenticity—deepens personal discipleship and reflects the mission and character of Christ.

3. Explore the Transformative Impact of Faith-Sharing on Individuals and Communities

Learners will be able to identify how intentional evangelism fosters spiritual growth, rekindles purpose, and builds relational bridges that lead others toward

Christ, while enriching the disciple's own journey.

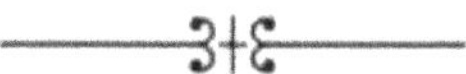

Salt and Light: A Narrative on Christian Discipleship and Evangelism

Marcus stared at his reflection in the subway window as the train rumbled through the underground tunnels of the city. Another Monday morning commute, another week of blending into the crowd. The sermon from yesterday still echoed in his mind: "You are the salt of the earth... You are the light of the world."

For fifteen years, Marcus had considered himself a devoted Christian. He attended church faithfully, participated in Bible studies, and even volunteered occasionally with the children's ministry. Yet something about yesterday's message on Matthew 5 had unsettled him. The pastor's words kept replaying in his mind: "Salt that stays in the shaker cannot flavor the world. Light hidden under a bowl illuminates nothing."

When had he become so comfortable keeping his faith contained within the church walls?

The Silent Witness

"Mind if I sit here?"

Marcus looked up to see a young woman gesturing to the empty seat beside him. He nodded and shifted to make room, then returned to scrolling through emails on his phone.

"Looks like it's going to rain all week," she remarked casually.

Under normal circumstances, Marcus would have offered a polite smile and minimal response before retreating back to the safety of his screen. But today, something prompted him to engage.

"They say we need the rain, though," he replied, putting his phone away. "I'm Marcus, by the way."

"Sophia," she said with a smile. "Do you make this commute often?"

What began as small talk gradually evolved into a deeper conversation. Sophia had recently moved to the city for work and was struggling with the isolation of urban life. As she spoke, Marcus felt a gentle nudge in his spirit—an opportunity opening before him.

"Actually, I found community through my church when I first moved here," he offered tentatively, waiting for the familiar awkward shift in conversation that often followed any mention of faith.

But instead of discomfort, he saw genuine interest spark in Sophia's eyes. "Really? I grew up attending church but haven't found one since moving. What's yours like?"

By the time they reached their stop, Marcus had not only told Sophia about his church but had offered to meet her in the lobby the following Sunday. As they parted ways, he felt an unexpected sense of fulfillment. Something as simple as mentioning his faith had created a connection that might not otherwise have formed.

The Cost of Silence

That evening, Marcus met his longtime friend David for their weekly dinner. David had been his roommate in college, and though they had once shared everything, including their Christian faith, David had gradually drifted away from his spiritual roots.

"So, how's life in the corporate jungle?" Marcus asked as they settled at their usual table.

"Same old rat race," David replied with a halfhearted smile. "But I'm up for promotion next month, so there's that."

As they caught up, Marcus couldn't help but notice the weariness behind his friend's eyes. Fifteen years of friendship, and yet Marcus had gradually stopped mentioning anything related to faith around David, afraid of creating tension in their relationship.

The pastor's words from Sunday surfaced again: "What good is salt that has lost its saltiness?"

"David," Marcus said suddenly, interrupting their usual conversation about sports, "are you happy?"

The question hung in the air between them, unexpected and weighty. David looked startled, then thoughtful.

"Honestly? Not really," he admitted. "Work is just work. My relationship with Megan is rocky. Sometimes I wonder what it's all for, you know?"

Marcus took a deep breath. "Remember how we used to talk about purpose in college? About how our faith gave everything meaning?"

David's expression softened. "Those were simpler times."

"Maybe," Marcus acknowledged, "but the truth hasn't changed. I've been a terrible friend by not sharing what still matters most to me, especially when I see you struggling."

To his surprise, David didn't pull away. "I've missed that part of my life," he confessed. "I've just been too proud to admit it."

As they spoke more openly than they had in years, Marcus realized how much his silence had cost both of them. He had been reluctant to risk their friendship by bringing up faith, but in reality, his silence had allowed a different kind of distance to grow between them.

A New Perspective

The following Sunday, Marcus felt unusually nervous as he waited in the church lobby. When Sophia appeared at the entrance, looking hesitant yet hopeful, he felt a surge of gratitude for the courage to have invited her.

During the service, he found himself experiencing worship through fresh eyes, aware of Sophia beside him encountering this community for the first time. The songs, the prayers, the message—all of it took on new significance when shared with someone discovering it anew.

Afterward, as they joined a group for coffee, Marcus introduced Sophia to others in the congregation. He watched as she was welcomed warmly, included in conversations, and even exchanged phone numbers with a few women close to her age.

"Thank you for inviting me," she told him earnestly as they parted ways. "I can't remember the last time I felt so... welcome somewhere."

On his drive home, Marcus reflected on how different his week had been since he'd started thinking intentionally about sharing his faith. It wasn't about grand evangelistic speeches or confrontational debates. It had been as simple as making his faith visible—removing the bowl from over his light.

The Ripple Effect

Three months later, Marcus sat in a small group meeting at church, listening as Sophia shared how finding this community had transformed her experience of the city.

"And it all started because Marcus mentioned church during a subway conversation," she said, smiling in his direction. "Sometimes the smallest invitation makes the biggest difference."

What Sophia didn't know—what Marcus himself was only beginning to realize—was how profoundly that simple act of evangelism had transformed his own discipleship journey. Sharing his faith had awakened something dormant within him, rekindling the sense of purpose and urgency that had characterized his early years as a believer.

David sat beside him in the group, still early in his journey back to faith but asking questions and engaging with Scripture in ways that reminded Marcus of their college days. Another colleague from work had joined them tonight, curious after noticing subtle changes in Marcus's approach to workplace challenges.

The pastor's words from that sermon now made perfect sense: evangelism wasn't an optional add-on to discipleship—it was essential to discipleship itself. In trying to share Christ with others, Marcus had found himself drawing closer to Christ.

The Integrated Life

One year after that fateful sermon, Marcus again found himself on the morning subway. The faces around him were no longer an anonymous crowd but a gathering of souls, each with stories, struggles, and spiritual journeys of their own.

Some of those faces had become familiar. There was Raj, from the financial district, who had started joining him for coffee and conversations about spirituality. There was Eleanor, the retired teacher who had initially been defensive about religion but now occasionally asked thoughtful questions about Marcus's "peace" in handling life's challenges.

His phone buzzed with a message from David: "Bringing two guys from work to the outreach event tonight. They're actually excited about it!"

Marcus smiled, remembering how nervous he had once been about simply mentioning his church to a stranger on the subway. Now, evangelism had become a natural extension of his life as a disciple—not a program or an obligation, but the overflow of a life transformed by grace and eager to share that transformation with others.

Jesus's words now resonated with new meaning: "Let your light shine before others, that they may see your good deeds and glorify your Father in heaven." The purpose of being salt and light wasn't self-promotion or even church growth—it was that others might encounter the glory of God.

In finding his voice to share his faith, Marcus had discovered the fullness of discipleship itself—following Jesus not just in personal piety but in mission and purpose. The light shining through him was illuminating his own path even as it guided others toward home.

Reflection

Chapter 8:

Discipling Others – Making Disciples

Scriptural Text:

He said unto them, Have ye received the Holy Ghost since ye believed? And they said unto him, We have not so much as heard whether there be any Holy Ghost.

Acts 19:2 (KJV)

And Saul arose from the earth; and when his eyes
were opened, he saw no man: but they led him by
the hand, and brought him into Damascus. 9 And
he was three days without sight, and neither did
eat nor drink. 10 And there was a certain disciple at
Damascus, named Ananias; and to him said the
Lord in a vision, Ananias. And he said, Behold, I am
here, Lord. 11 And the Lord said unto him, Arise,
and go into the street which is called Straight, and
enquire in the house of Judas for one called Saul, of
Tarsus: for, behold, he prayeth, 12 And hath seen in
a vision a man named Ananias coming in, and

putting his hand on him, that he might receive his sight. 13 Then Ananias answered, Lord, I have heard by many of this man, how much evil he hath done to thy saints at Jerusalem:

Acts 9:8-13 (KJV)

Learning Objectives:

1. Understand the Relational Nature of Christian Discipleship as Modeled by Jesus

Learners will be able to explain how Jesus' example of walking alongside His disciples demonstrates that spiritual growth is nurtured through authentic relationships, shared experiences, and mutual trust.

2. Recognize the Importance of Trust and Vulnerability in Fostering Spiritual Transformation

Learners will be able to describe how intentionality, empathy, and openness build trust within discipleship relationships, creating safe spaces for encouragement, accountability, and personal growth.

3. Apply Principles of Relational Discipleship to Community Engagement and Gospel Witness

Learners will be able to identify ways to extend discipleship beyond church walls by building bridges of trust, serving others with compassion, and reflecting Christ's love through everyday interactions.

The Role of Relationships and Trust in Christian Discipleship

The journey of Christian discipleship is a transformative calling that compels believers to follow Jesus, embody His teachings, and serve others with love and humility. While discipleship demands personal commitment and surrender to Christ, it is not meant to be an isolated pursuit. At its heart, Christian discipleship is deeply relational, emphasizing the importance of building interpersonal connections and fostering trust within the body of Christ and beyond. By investing in relationships and nurturing trust, disciples fulfill their calling to reflect God's love and advance His kingdom through authentic community.

Samantha had always loved the idea of discipleship. As a passionate believer, she was eager to grow in her faith and share the gospel with others. Yet, she often found herself feeling disconnected from those around her, hesitant to open up or engage deeply with others. She wondered whether discipleship was simply a matter of personal spiritual growth or if it involved something more—something she was missing.

One Sunday morning, her pastor preached a message on the power of relationships in discipleship. He explained how Jesus Himself modeled relational discipleship, choosing twelve ordinary men to walk alongside Him, learn from Him, and ultimately spread His message of salvation. The pastor emphasized that discipleship flourishes in the context of community, where believers can encourage, challenge, and support one another.

Samantha left the service with a newfound sense of curiosity and conviction. Could building relationships be the missing piece in her discipleship journey? She resolved to explore this idea further, stepping out of her comfort zone to engage with others in ways that mirrored Christ's example.

Relational Discipleship: Following the Example of Jesus

Jesus' ministry was fundamentally relational. He did not carry out His mission in isolation; instead, He surrounded Himself with people, investing deeply in their lives. He chose twelve disciples to be His closest companions, teaching them through shared experiences, conversations, and acts of service. Jesus fostered trust with His disciples, inviting them to witness His miracles, participate in His ministry, and learn from His example.

In John 15:15, Jesus tells His disciples, “I no longer call you servants, because a servant does not know his master’s business. Instead, I have called you friends.” This statement reflects the relational nature of discipleship—a connection built not on hierarchy or obligation but on mutual love and trust. Samantha realized that true discipleship involved walking alongside others, creating spaces where vulnerability and trust could flourish.

As Samantha began to invest in relationships, she joined a small group at her church. At first, it was daunting to share her thoughts and struggles with others, but she quickly discovered the beauty of authentic community. Through these connections, she experienced the encouragement and accountability that come from walking with fellow believers.

She saw how discipleship was not limited to personal spiritual growth but extended to helping others grow in their faith as well.

The Importance of Trust in Discipleship Relationships

Trust is the foundation of any meaningful relationship, and it is particularly vital in discipleship. Without trust, relationships remain superficial, unable to support the depth of spiritual growth and transformation that discipleship requires. Jesus demonstrated the importance of trust in His relationships with the disciples, inviting them into His inner circle and entrusting them with His mission.

Samantha learned that building trust involved intentionality and vulnerability. Trust was not something that happened overnight; it was cultivated through consistent actions, honesty, and empathy. She began to listen more attentively to others, seeking to understand their experiences and perspectives. She shared her own challenges and victories, allowing others to see her authentic self.

One of Samantha's most transformative moments came when a fellow small group member confided in her about a personal struggle. Instead of offering quick solutions, Samantha chose to listen and empathize, creating a safe space for her friend to share openly. This experience deepened their bond and reminded Samantha that discipleship was not just about teaching or guiding others—it was about walking alongside them in their joys and trials.

Encouraging Growth Through Relationships

Building interpersonal relationships and trust in discipleship is not merely about fostering connection; it is about encouraging spiritual growth and transformation. In Proverbs 27:17, we read, "As iron sharpens iron, so one person sharpens another." This verse underscores the idea that relationships challenge and refine us, helping us grow in our faith and character.

Through her small group and other relational interactions, Samantha saw firsthand how relationships could inspire growth. Her friends encouraged her to study Scripture more deeply, step out in faith, and serve others boldly. They held her accountable when she struggled and celebrated her successes when she persevered. In turn, Samantha began to do the same for them, recognizing that discipleship was a reciprocal journey.

Samantha also learned that relationships extended beyond the confines of church walls. She felt compelled to reach out to those in her community who did not yet know Christ, building bridges of trust and understanding. She volunteered at a local shelter, forging connections with individuals facing hardship. Through these relationships, she found opportunities to share the gospel and reflect God's love in tangible ways.

The Challenges and Rewards of Relational Discipleship

As Samantha embraced relational discipleship, she discovered that it was not without challenges. Building trust and fostering connections required time, effort, and patience. Relationships could be messy and unpredictable, often demanding grace and forgiveness. Yet, she also found that the rewards far outweighed the difficulties.

Through her relational discipleship journey, Samantha experienced the joy of seeing others grow in their faith. She witnessed lives transformed by the love of Christ and felt the deep fulfillment that comes from being part of God's redemptive work. She realized that discipleship was not a solitary endeavor but a shared journey that reflected the relational nature of God Himself.

Conclusion

Christian discipleship is not an isolated pursuit but a deeply relational journey that calls believers to build connections and foster trust with others. By following Jesus' example, investing in relationships, and cultivating trust, disciples create spaces for spiritual growth, encouragement, and transformation. Samantha's journey of relational discipleship reminds us that we are called not only to follow Christ individually but to walk alongside others, reflecting His love and advancing His kingdom through authentic community.

Relationships and trust are the lifeblood of discipleship, enabling believers to grow in their faith and impact the lives of others. While the path may be challenging, the rewards are immeasurable—a life enriched by meaningful connections, a heart aligned with God's will, and the privilege of participating in His redemptive work. As disciples embrace the relational nature of their calling, they embody the love of Christ and fulfill His command to make disciples of all nations.

Reflection

Reflection

Chapter 9:

Challenges in Discipleship

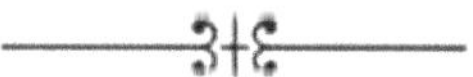

Scriptural Text:

For first of all, when ye come together in the
church, I hear that there be divisions among you;
and I partly believe it. 19 For there must be also
heresies among you, that they which are approved
may be made manifest among you. 20 When ye
come together therefore into one place, this is not
to eat the Lord's supper. 21 For in eating every one
taketh before other his own supper: and one is
hungry, and another is drunken. 22 What? have ye
not houses to eat and to drink in? or despise ye the
church of God, and shame them that have not?
what shall I say to you? shall I praise you in this? I
praise you not.

I Corinthians 11:18 (KJV)

Learning Objectives:

1. Recognize Common Challenges in the Discipleship Journey and Their Role in Spiritual Growth

Learners will be able to identify relational conflict, internal doubt, and personal trials as integral aspects of discipleship, and explain how these experiences contribute to perseverance, character development, and deeper faith.

2. Understand the Importance of Reconciliation, Trust in God, and Community Support in Navigating Adversity

Learners will be able to describe how humility, prayer, and relational accountability help disciples overcome obstacles and remain faithful to their calling.

3. Apply Biblical Principles to Embrace the Refining Process of Discipleship

Learners will be able to articulate how Scripture guides believers through hardship, encouraging them to view challenges as opportunities for transformation and to reflect Christ's love more fully in their lives and ministries.

Overcoming Challenges in the Journey of Christian Discipleship

The path of Christian discipleship is marked by joy and growth, yet it is not devoid of challenges. Jesus Himself warned that following Him would require perseverance, sacrifice, and faithfulness in the face of adversity. Whether it's conflicts with others, internal struggles, or trials that seem insurmountable, disciples must learn to navigate these difficulties with courage and trust in God's guidance.

For Mark, a dedicated believer and mentor in his church, the journey of discipleship had always been both deeply rewarding and deeply challenging. He cherished his role in mentoring younger Christians and fostering their growth in faith. However, as the years passed, Mark found himself grappling with a series of obstacles that tested his commitment to the discipleship journey.

Conflict in Relationships: The Call to Reconciliation

Mark's first challenge emerged in the form of a conflict with a close friend and fellow believer, James. What began as a simple disagreement over ministry decisions quickly escalated into tension and misunderstandings. Mark felt frustrated and betrayed, unsure how to approach reconciliation.

In moments of conflict, disciples are called to reflect Christ's example of humility, love, and forgiveness. Matthew 5:23-24 teaches,

“If you are offering your gift at the altar and there remember that your brother or sister has something against you, leave your gift there in front of the altar. First go and be reconciled to them; then come and offer your gift.” Mark knew these words well, yet putting them into practice required swallowing his pride and seeking peace.

One evening, after much prayer, Mark reached out to James, inviting him for coffee. Their conversation began with awkwardness but soon turned into a heartfelt exchange. Mark apologized for his part in the conflict, and James did the same. They realized that their shared commitment to Christ far outweighed their differences. This experience not only restored their friendship but also deepened Mark’s understanding of reconciliation as an essential aspect of discipleship.

Internal Struggles: Trusting God in the Midst of Doubt

While external conflicts can challenge discipleship, internal struggles often cut even deeper. For Mark, doubts and insecurities began to creep into his heart during a season of personal loss. The passing of a loved one left him questioning God's plan and wondering whether he was truly making a difference as a disciple.

In times of doubt, disciples are reminded of the importance of anchoring their faith in God's promises. Psalm 34:18 offers comfort, stating, "The Lord is close to the brokenhearted and saves those who are crushed in spirit." Mark found solace in these words, turning to prayer and Scripture as sources of strength.

One morning, during his quiet time with God, Mark came across the story of Thomas, the disciple who doubted Jesus' resurrection. In John 20:27, Jesus said to Thomas, "Stop doubting and believe." This gentle yet firm invitation resonated deeply with Mark. He realized that doubt was not a sign of failure but an opportunity to draw closer to God and seek His truth.

Through prayer, journaling, and conversations with trusted mentors, Mark began to process his doubts and renew his trust in God. He learned that discipleship is not about having all the answers but about remaining faithful in the midst of uncertainty. His doubts transformed into a deeper reliance on God's grace and a renewed passion for serving others.

Facing Trials: Finding Strength in Community

The journey of discipleship also includes seasons of trials and challenges that test one's endurance. For Mark, this came in the form of burnout. Balancing work, ministry, and family responsibilities left him feeling drained and overwhelmed. He began to question whether he could continue pouring into others while his own spiritual well-being seemed to suffer.

In these moments, the importance of community becomes evident. Ecclesiastes 4:9-10 reminds us, “Two are better than one, because they have a good return for their labor: If either of them falls down, one can help the other up.” Mark’s small group noticed his weariness and stepped in to support him. They prayed for him, offered words of encouragement, and even helped lighten his ministry load.

One of Mark’s closest friends, Sarah, reminded him of Jesus’ invitation in Matthew 11:28-30: “Come to me, all you who are weary and burdened, and I will give you rest.” These words served as a reminder that discipleship is not about striving in one’s own strength but about leaning on God and allowing Him to carry the burdens.

With the support of his community, Mark took intentional steps to rest and recharge. He carved out time for solitude with God, seeking His presence and peace. This season of renewal allowed Mark to return to his ministry with a refreshed spirit and a deeper appreciation for the role of community in discipleship.

Perseverance and Growth: Embracing the Refining Process

As Mark reflected on his journey, he realized that each challenge he faced had a purpose in shaping his character and deepening his faith. Romans 5:3-4 states, "Not only so, but we also glory in our sufferings, because we know that suffering produces perseverance; perseverance, character; and character, hope." Mark's experiences of conflict, doubt, and trials were not obstacles to discipleship—they were integral parts of the refining process.

Through these challenges, Mark grew in humility, patience, and resilience. He learned to rely not on his own strength but on God's power working through him. He also discovered that discipleship is not a solitary journey but one that thrives in the context of relationships and community.

As he continued to mentor others, Mark shared his experiences openly, offering encouragement and wisdom to those facing similar challenges. He reminded them that difficulties are not signs of failure but opportunities to trust God more deeply and grow in faith.

Conclusion

Christian discipleship is a journey filled with both joy and challenges. Conflicts, internal struggles, and trials are inevitable, yet they are also opportunities for growth, transformation, and deeper reliance on God. Mark's story illustrates how disciples can navigate these difficulties through reconciliation, trust in God, and the support of community.

Ultimately, the challenges of discipleship are not roadblocks but stepping stones on the path to spiritual maturity. As disciples embrace the refining process, they reflect Christ's love and grace more fully, becoming vessels for His redemptive work in the world. Through perseverance, humility, and faith, they discover the beauty of a life surrendered to God—a life that glorifies Him even in the midst of difficulties.

Reflection

Chapter 10:

Stewardship - Managing God's Resources: Time, Talent and Treasure

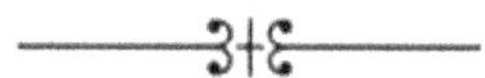

Scriptural Text:

His lord said unto him, Well done, good and faithful servant; thou hast been faithful over a few things, I will make thee ruler over many things: enter thou into the joy of thy lord.

Matthew 25:23 (KJV)

Neither was there any among them that lacked: for as many as were possessors of lands or houses sold them, and brought the prices of the things that were sold,

Acts 4:34 (KJV)

Learning Objectives:

1. Understand the Biblical Foundation and Spiritual Significance of Stewardship in Discipleship

Learners will be able to explain how managing money, time, and talent as entrusted resources reflects a disciple's relationship with God and contributes to the advancement of His kingdom.

2. Apply Principles of Faithful Stewardship to Everyday Life and Ministry

Learners will be able to identify practical ways to align financial decisions, time management, and personal gifts with God's purposes, using intentionality, generosity, and service as expressions of worship.

3. Recognize the Challenges and Growth Opportunities in the Stewardship Journey

Learners will be able to describe how perseverance, community support, and reliance on God's grace help disciples overcome obstacles and deepen their commitment to faithful stewardship.

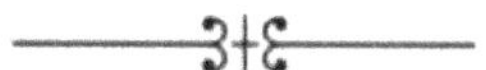

Stewardship and Discipleship: Honoring God Through Resources

Christian discipleship is a transformative journey that calls believers to follow Jesus wholeheartedly and reflect His love, character, and teachings. Embedded within this journey is the vital principle of stewardship—the responsibility to manage the resources God has entrusted to us in a way that glorifies Him and advances His kingdom. Whether it is money, time, or talent, disciples are called to recognize these resources as gifts from God and use them faithfully for His purposes.

For Rebecca, stewardship was an idea she had encountered often in church teachings, yet it remained somewhat abstract in her daily life. As a young professional striving to balance her career, family, and faith, Rebecca often felt overwhelmed by the demands on her resources. She questioned whether she was truly honoring God with her finances, time, and unique abilities. One Sunday, as she listened to a sermon on stewardship, the pastor shared a powerful statement: "As disciples of Christ, we are not owners but caretakers of God's blessings. How we use those blessings reflects our relationship with Him."

Rebecca left the service with a sense of conviction and curiosity. She resolved to explore what it meant to be a good steward and to align her discipleship journey with this important calling.

Money: Faithful Stewardship of Financial Resources

The Bible speaks extensively about the stewardship of money, reminding believers that wealth is a gift from God and should be used wisely and generously. In Matthew

6:24, Jesus warns, "You cannot serve both God and money," highlighting the importance of prioritizing God over material possessions. For Rebecca, this teaching resonated deeply as she reflected on her own financial choices.

Rebecca decided to reassess her spending habits and create a budget that reflected her commitment to stewardship. She set aside a portion of her income for tithing, recognizing that giving to her church and charitable causes was an act of worship and trust in God's provision. She also began to view her spending through the lens of intentionality, choosing to support businesses that aligned with her values and avoiding unnecessary purchases.

One of Rebecca's most transformative moments came when she participated in a community outreach program that provided financial assistance to families in need. As she witnessed the impact of generosity firsthand, she realized that stewardship was not about accumulating wealth for personal comfort but about using resources to bless others and advance God's kingdom.

Rebecca found encouragement in 2 Corinthians 9:7, which states, "Each of you should give what you have decided in your heart to give, not reluctantly or under compulsion, for God loves a cheerful giver." This verse reminded her that stewardship was an opportunity to express gratitude and trust in God's provision.

Time: Prioritizing What Matters

Time is one of the most precious resources God has given us, yet it is often taken for granted or spent on pursuits that distract from His purposes. Rebecca struggled with this aspect of stewardship, feeling torn between the demands of her busy schedule and her desire to grow in her faith.

In Ephesians 5:15-16, Paul encourages believers to "be very careful, then, how you live—not as unwise but as wise, making the most of every opportunity, because the days are evil." Rebecca pondered these words, realizing that good stewardship of time required intentionality and focus on what truly mattered.

She began by evaluating her daily routines, identifying activities that consumed time without adding value to her discipleship journey. Rebecca set aside dedicated moments for prayer, Scripture reading, and serving others, recognizing that these practices were essential to her spiritual growth. She also learned to say no to commitments that distracted from her priorities, trusting that God would guide her in using her time effectively.

One evening, Rebecca volunteered at a local shelter, assisting with meal preparation and spending time with residents. As she listened to their stories and offered encouragement, she felt a profound sense of purpose and fulfillment. She realized that time spent serving others was not wasted—it was an investment in relationships and an expression of God's love.

Rebecca also discovered the importance of rest as an act of stewardship. She embraced the biblical principle of Sabbath, taking time to recharge physically, emotionally, and spiritually. By prioritizing rest, she found renewed energy to serve God and others more effectively.

Talent: Using Gifts to Serve

Every disciple is uniquely gifted with talents and abilities that can be used to glorify God and bless others. In 1 Peter 4:10, believers are instructed, "Each of you should use whatever gift you have received to serve others, as faithful stewards of God's grace in its various forms." For Rebecca, stewardship of talent was both exciting and challenging, as she sought to identify and use her gifts in meaningful ways.

Rebecca discovered her passion for music and storytelling; talents she had often considered hobbies rather than tools for discipleship. Encouraged by her church community, she began to lead worship and share personal testimonies during events. These opportunities allowed her to connect with others on a deeper level, inspiring them to pursue their own discipleship journeys.

Stewarding talent also involved humility and a willingness to grow. Rebecca took time to hone her skills, recognizing that excellence in her abilities was a way to honor God. She sought mentorship from experienced leaders, learning how to use her gifts more effectively for ministry.

Through her experiences, Rebecca realized that talent was not about personal recognition but about pointing others to Christ. She found joy in using her gifts to bring people together, foster worship, and encourage spiritual growth. Her talents became a powerful tool for advancing God's kingdom and reflecting His grace.

Challenges and Growth in Stewardship

Rebecca's journey of stewardship was not without challenges. She faced moments of doubt, questioning whether her efforts truly made a difference. She struggled with balancing her resources and sometimes felt overwhelmed by the demands of discipleship.

In these moments, Rebecca turned to prayer and sought wisdom from Scripture. She found comfort in Matthew 25:21, where Jesus commends faithful stewardship, saying, "Well done, good and faithful servant!" These words reminded her that stewardship was not about perfection but about faithfulness and trust in God's guidance.

Rebecca also leaned on her community for support, sharing her struggles and seeking encouragement from fellow believers. Together, they celebrated victories, prayed through challenges, and held one another accountable in their stewardship journeys.

Conclusion

Christian discipleship calls believers to be faithful stewards of God's resources—money, time, and talent. Rebecca's story illustrates how stewardship is not merely a responsibility but a profound act of worship, gratitude, and trust in God. By managing these resources intentionally and generously, disciples honor God and participate in His redemptive work.

Stewardship is a lifelong journey that requires humility, perseverance, and reliance on God's grace. As disciples embrace this calling, they discover the joy of reflecting God's character, blessing others, and advancing His kingdom. Through faithful stewardship, they fulfill their purpose as caretakers of God's blessings and experience the richness of life in Him.

Reflection

Chapter 11:

Forgiveness and Healing

Scriptural Text:

For if ye forgive men their trespasses, your heavenly Father will also forgive you: 15 But if ye forgive not men their trespasses, neither will your Father forgive your trespasses.

Matthew 6:14-15 (KJV)

Learning Objectives:

1. Understand the Biblical Foundations of Healing and Forgiveness as Essential to Discipleship

Learners will be able to explain how healing and forgiveness reflect God's character, support spiritual freedom, and are vital to a disciple's relationship with Christ and others.

2. Recognize the Transformative Impact of Healing and Forgiveness on Personal and Communal Relationships

Learners will be able to describe how practicing healing and forgiveness restores broken relationships, fosters unity within the body of Christ, and encourages reconciliation in broader social contexts.

3. Apply Principles of Healing and Forgiveness to Real-Life Challenges with Humility and Perseverance

Learners will be able to identify practical steps for addressing unresolved pain, extending grace, and navigating relational conflict, while relying on Scripture, prayer, and community support.

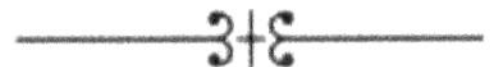

Healing and Forgiveness: Cornerstones of Christian Discipleship

Christian discipleship is an invitation to follow Jesus wholeheartedly, embracing His teachings and embodying His love. Central to this journey are the transformative principles of healing and forgiveness. These cornerstones not only reflect God's character but also enable disciples to walk in freedom, restore relationships, and advance His kingdom with compassion and grace. By practicing healing and forgiveness, disciples emulate Christ's example, experiencing personal renewal and fostering unity within the body of Christ.

Martha's journey as a disciple had always been deeply rooted in her desire to serve others. She volunteered at her local church, led small group Bible studies, and participated in community outreach programs. Yet, beneath the surface of her outward dedication, Martha carried the weight of unresolved pain—a fractured relationship with her younger sister, Anna. Years earlier, a misunderstanding had driven a wedge between them, leaving Martha with lingering hurt and bitterness.

Despite her efforts to suppress these feelings, Martha began to notice how they affected her interactions with others. She found it difficult to extend grace to those who disappointed her and often felt disconnected during worship. It was during a Sunday sermon on forgiveness that Martha felt a conviction in her heart. The pastor shared the words of Jesus from Matthew 6:14-15: "For if you forgive other people when they sin against you, your heavenly Father will also forgive you. But if you do not forgive others their sins, your Father will not forgive your sins."

Martha realized that healing and forgiveness were not optional aspects of discipleship—they were essential to her relationship with God and her ability to reflect His love.

The Healing Power of Christ

Healing is a recurring theme in the life and ministry of Jesus. From physical ailments to emotional wounds, Jesus demonstrated His power and compassion by bringing restoration to those in need. In Matthew 11:28-30, He invites the weary and burdened to come to Him, promising rest for their souls. This invitation extends to all disciples, offering hope and renewal in the midst of pain.

For Martha, healing began with acknowledging her hurt and bringing it before God in prayer. She realized that true healing required honesty—both with herself and with God. As she poured out her pain to Him, she felt a sense of release, as if the weight she had been carrying was slowly lifting. Through Scripture, Martha was reminded that God is "close to the brokenhearted and saves those who are crushed in spirit" (Psalm 34:18).

In her journey toward healing, Martha also sought wise counsel from a trusted mentor at her church. Her mentor encouraged her to reflect on Jesus' example of compassion and to allow His love to mend the broken places in her heart. This process was not instantaneous; it required patience and a willingness to trust God's timing. Yet, Martha began to experience the peace that comes from surrendering her pain to the One who heals.

Forgiveness: A Reflection of God's Grace

Forgiveness is one of the most profound expressions of God's grace, and it is a defining characteristic of Christian discipleship. Jesus exemplified forgiveness in His interactions with others, extending mercy to those who wronged Him and teaching His followers to do the same. On the cross, He prayed, "Father, forgive them, for they do not know what they are doing" (Luke 23:34), demonstrating the depth of His love and the power of forgiveness.

For Martha, the call to forgive Anna was both challenging and transformative. She wrestled with feelings of resentment, questioning whether forgiveness was truly possible after years of estrangement. Yet, as she reflected on Jesus' teachings, she realized that forgiveness was not about condoning wrongdoing or erasing the past—it was about releasing the hold that bitterness had on her heart.

Martha found encouragement in Colossians 3:13, which states, "Bear with each other and forgive one another if any of you has a grievance against someone. Forgive as the Lord forgave you." These words reminded her that forgiveness was an act of obedience and a reflection of the forgiveness she had received from God.

With much prayer and humility, Martha reached out to Anna, expressing her desire to reconcile. Their initial conversation was hesitant, filled with both apologies and tears. Over time, as they continued to communicate and rebuild trust, Martha experienced the freedom that comes from forgiveness. She discovered that forgiveness was not only a gift to Anna but also a gift to herself, allowing her to move forward with a renewed sense of peace.

Healing and Forgiveness in Community

The principles of healing and forgiveness extend beyond individual relationships—they are vital to the health and unity of the Christian community. Disciples are called to be peacemakers, fostering reconciliation and embodying God's love within the body of Christ.

In Ephesians 4:31-32, Paul urges believers, "Get rid of all bitterness, rage and anger, brawling and slander, along with every form of malice. Be kind and compassionate to one another, forgiving each other, just as in Christ God forgave you." These words highlight the importance of creating a culture of grace, where healing and forgiveness are practiced collectively.

Martha's journey of healing and forgiveness inspired others in her church community to address their own unresolved conflicts. She shared her testimony during a small group meeting, encouraging her fellow believers to seek reconciliation in their relationships. Her vulnerability and willingness to forgive became a powerful example of God's transformative work.

Challenges and Growth in Healing and Forgiveness

The journey of healing and forgiveness is not without challenges. Disciples may encounter resistance, misunderstandings, or the temptation to revert to old patterns of hurt and resentment. Yet, these challenges are opportunities for growth and reliance on God's grace.

Martha faced moments of doubt and frustration as she navigated her relationship with Anna. There were times when old wounds resurfaced, threatening to overshadow their progress. In these moments, Martha turned to prayer and Scripture, reminding herself of God's faithfulness and the call to persevere in love.

Through her experiences, Martha learned that healing and forgiveness are ongoing processes. They require humility, patience, and a willingness to trust God's redemptive work. She also discovered that these principles are not limited to personal relationships—they extend to broader contexts, such as social and cultural divisions. As disciples, the call to healing and forgiveness challenges believers to be agents of reconciliation in a fractured world.

Conclusion

Christian discipleship is a journey of transformation, marked by the principles of healing and forgiveness. These cornerstones enable disciples to walk in freedom, restore relationships, and reflect God's love in a broken world. Martha's story illustrates the power of healing and forgiveness to bring renewal, both individually and within the community of faith.

As disciples embrace the call to healing and forgiveness, they embody the heart of Jesus, offering compassion and grace to those around them. While the journey may be challenging, it is also deeply rewarding, leading to personal growth, restored relationships, and unity within the body of Christ. Through healing and forgiveness, disciples participate in God's redemptive work, shining His light in a world in need of hope.

Reflection

Chapter 12:

The Rewards of Discipleship

Scriptural Text

And he saith unto them, Follow me, and I will make you fishers of men.

Matthew 4:19 (KJV)

Be ye followers of me, even as I also am of Christ.

1 Corinthians 11:1 (KJV)

Learning Objectives:

1. Understand the Relationship Between Following Christ and Experiencing True Joy

Learners will be able to explain how personal commitment to Jesus, rooted in trust and obedience, leads to a joy that transcends circumstances and deepens through spiritual intimacy.

2. Recognize the Transformative Power of Discipleship in Shaping Character and Purpose

Learners will be able to describe how abiding in Christ and serving others cultivates spiritual growth, reveals personal gifts, and fosters a fulfilling life aligned with God's will.

3. Apply Biblical Principles to Persevere Through Challenges with Faith and Joy

Learners will be able to identify how trials and setbacks serve as opportunities for maturity, and how disciples can draw strength from Scripture, prayer, and community to remain faithful and hopeful.

Joy in the Journey: The Fulfillment of Christian Discipleship

Christian discipleship is more than a commitment—it is a lifelong journey of following Jesus, growing in His teachings, and experiencing the deep joy and fulfillment that come from living in close relationship with Him. At its core, discipleship is an invitation to abundant life, marked by purpose, transformation, and the profound love of God. As disciples learn to trust in Christ, walk in obedience, and reflect His character, they discover the true joy that transcends circumstances and the fulfillment that comes from aligning their lives with God's will.

For Jonathan, the idea of discipleship had always been a familiar one. Raised in a Christian home, he attended church regularly and participated in various ministries. Yet, his faith felt more like a routine than a vibrant relationship with Christ. Jonathan longed for something deeper—a sense of purpose and joy that went beyond surface-level religion. Little did he know that his journey of discipleship would lead him to experience the abundant life Jesus promised in John 10:10: "I have come that they may have life, and have it to the full."

Following Christ: The Source of True Joy

The journey of discipleship begins with a simple yet profound decision: to follow Jesus. In Matthew 4:19, Jesus calls His first disciples, saying, "Come, follow me, and I will send you out to fish for people." This call is both an invitation and a promise—an invitation to walk with Christ and a promise of transformation and purpose.

For Jonathan, following Christ became a personal commitment during a retreat he attended with his church. As he listened to a message about Jesus' invitation to "take up their cross and follow Me" (Matthew 16:24), Jonathan felt a stirring in his heart. He realized that discipleship was not about adhering to a checklist of religious practices but about surrendering his life to Jesus and trusting Him as the source of true joy.

Jonathan's decision to follow Christ marked a turning point in his life. He began to spend time in prayer and Scripture, seeking to know Jesus more intimately. As he grew in his relationship with Christ, Jonathan experienced a joy that was not dependent on his circumstances but rooted in the presence of God. This joy became a wellspring of strength, sustaining him through challenges and inspiring him to share his faith with others.

Growing in Christ: Transformation and Fulfillment

Discipleship is not a one-time decision but a lifelong process of growth and transformation. In John 15:5, Jesus uses the metaphor of a vine and branches to describe the importance of abiding in Him: "I am the vine; you are the branches. If you remain in me and I in you, you will bear much fruit; apart from me you can do nothing." This abiding relationship is the foundation of spiritual growth, enabling disciples to bear fruit in their lives and experience the fulfillment of living in alignment with God's purposes.

Jonathan discovered the joy of growth as he immersed himself in God's Word and sought to apply its truths to his life. He joined a small group at his church, where he found encouragement and accountability from fellow believers. Through their discussions and shared experiences, Jonathan learned to navigate the challenges of discipleship, from overcoming doubt to resisting temptation. Each step of growth deepened his understanding of God's character and His plan for Jonathan's life.

One of the most fulfilling aspects of Jonathan's journey was witnessing the transformation that occurred as he grew in Christ. He noticed changes in his attitudes, priorities, and relationships. Where he once struggled with anger and impatience, he began to exhibit the fruits of the Spirit—love, joy, peace, patience, kindness, goodness, faithfulness, gentleness, and self-control (Galatians 5:22-23). These changes were not the result of his own efforts but the work of the Holy Spirit within him, shaping him to reflect the image of Christ.

Serving Others: Joy in Purpose

As Jonathan continued to grow in his faith, he felt a strong desire to serve others. He came to understand that discipleship was not just about personal transformation but about living out the love of Christ in tangible ways. In Matthew 20:28, Jesus declares, "The Son of Man did not come to be served, but to serve, and to give His life as a ransom for many." This servant-hearted attitude became a guiding principle for Jonathan as he sought to make a difference in the lives of those around him.

Jonathan began volunteering at a local shelter, where he helped provide meals and companionship to individuals experiencing homelessness. At first, he felt hesitant and unsure of how he could make an impact. However, as he interacted with the shelter's guests, Jonathan discovered the joy of serving others and being part of God's redemptive work. Each smile, conversation, and shared moment reminded him of the value of every individual and the privilege of reflecting Christ's love.

Serving others also deepened Jonathan's sense of purpose and fulfillment. He realized that his talents, time, and resources were gifts from God, entrusted to him for the benefit of others. By using these gifts to bless and uplift others, Jonathan experienced the joy of living a life that mattered—a life that pointed others to Jesus.

Overcoming Challenges: Joy in Perseverance

The journey of discipleship is not without challenges. Disciples face trials, opposition, and moments of doubt that test their faith and resolve. Yet, it is often in these challenges that disciples experience the greatest growth and joy. In James 1:2-4, believers are encouraged to "consider it pure joy... whenever you face trials of many kinds, because you know that the testing of your faith produces perseverance. Let perseverance finish its work so that you may be mature and complete, not lacking anything."

Jonathan encountered his share of difficulties along the way, from strained relationships to unexpected setbacks. There were moments when he felt discouraged and questioned whether his efforts were making a difference. However, he found strength in God's promises and the support of his church community. Through prayer, Scripture, and the encouragement of others, Jonathan learned to persevere with faith and trust in God's plan.

One of the most powerful lessons Jonathan learned was that joy is not the absence of challenges but the presence of Christ in the midst of them. As he walked through trials, he experienced the peace and comfort of God's presence, which sustained him and reminded him of the hope he had in Christ.

Conclusion

Christian discipleship is a journey of joy and fulfillment, rooted in the decision to follow Jesus, grow in His teachings, and serve others with love. Jonathan's story illustrates the transformative power of discipleship, from the joy of abiding in Christ to the fulfillment of living out His purpose. Along the way, he discovered that true joy is not found in external circumstances but in the deep, abiding relationship with the One who calls us to abundant life.

As disciples embrace the call to follow and grow in Christ, they experience the joy of transformation, the fulfillment of purpose, and the hope of eternal life. This journey is not without challenges, but it is marked by the presence and faithfulness of God, who walks with His disciples every step of the way. Through discipleship, believers are invited into a life that reflects God's glory and brings His love to a world in need.

Reflection

Reflection

About the Author

Psalm 37:23 says, "The steps of a good man are ordered by the Lord..." This scripture perfectly encapsulates the life and ministry of Bishop Larry Lawrence Brandon, a devoted servant of God and humanity. As the Founder of Praise Temple, one of the most vibrant congregations in the Shreveport-Bossier City area, Bishop Brandon has spent decades building a ministry that is dynamic, impactful, and community-focused. He also serves as the Third Presiding Bishop of the Full Gospel Baptist Church Fellowship International, founded by his pastor, Bishop Paul S. Morton, Sr., and now led by Bishop J. Warren Walker. His leadership extends beyond the pulpit, having served as the Chairman of the Tehillah Music Group and contributed to many other initiatives within the Fellowship. His influence as a minister, mentor, counselor, speaker, radio personality, and spiritual father has shaped countless lives. Additionally, he founded L.L. Brandon Ministries, Inc., through which he consults for nonprofits and small businesses, helping them thrive and expand their community impact.

In 2022, Bishop Brandon was presented as the third pastor of the historic Evergreen Missionary Baptist Church in Oakland, California. His visionary leadership and Spirit-led teachings have inspired, instructed, and transformed lives, leading the congregation and the community into a new season of growth and spiritual renewal.

A United States Air Force Veteran, Bishop Brandon's dedication to service reaches beyond the church. His leadership in the community includes serving as a Life Member of the historic Alpha Phi Alpha Fraternity, Inc., 100 Black Men of the Bay area, former Chairman of the Shreveport Regional Airport Authority Board, from which he stepped down to accept an appointment to the Louisiana State Ethics Board, elected by the Louisiana House of Representatives. His chaplaincy work spans several key institutions, including the Louisiana State Police, Public Safety Services, Caddo Parish District Attorney's Office, Bossier Parish District Attorney's Office, Shreveport Fire Department, and the Shreveport City Marshal's Office.

Bishop Brandon was honored with an invitation to serve as Guest Chaplain for the United States House of Representatives in Washington, D.C., at the request of the 56th House Speaker, the Honorable James Michael Johnson. Also, he was inducted into an elite group of religious leaders and awarded the Honorary Guest Chaplain Pin for his service to the House of Representatives. Moreover, Bishop Brandon received the distinguished invitation to serve as Guest Chaplain for the United States Senate, extended by Louisiana Senator Bill Cassidy, further recognizing his commitment to faith and public service at the highest levels of government.

Bishop Brandon is actively involved in civic engagement as a co-founder and Former Board Member of the Step Forward Children's Education Initiative, Adult Prisoner's Reentry Initiative, and the Rotary Club of Shreveport. His extensive board memberships and commissions reflect his commitment to service. He is the Managing Partner of Brandon Group International LLC, he leads as the Facility Administrator and Center Director of the L.L. Brandon III Transitional Home for Boys, and the Chief Executive Officer and Executive Director of the Northwest Louisiana Community Development Corporation. Bishop Brandon also serves as the President/CEO of Evergreen Terrace Housing Corporation, Evergreen Annexed, Inc., President of the Evergreen Community Development Corporation.

In 2000, he completed his Episcopal Studies and Continuing Education at the prestigious Joint College of African American Bishops in Vatican City, Rome, Italy, and completed the Summer Leader Program at Harvard Divinity. In 2005, Bishop Larry Brandon served as Chancellor of the University Christian Preparatory School in Shreveport, Louisiana, overseeing educational programs for students from Pre-K3 through 12th grade and a Certified Adverse Childhood Experience (ACE) Educator. His commitment to education culminated in earning his Doctorate of Ministry in Church Ministries and Leadership from Oral Roberts University.

In addition to his pastoral duties, Bishop Brandon is a prolific author. His groundbreaking books include *From Private Pain to Public Victory*, *Treasures in the Darkness*, *Holiness Is Still Right*, *A Faith That Feels Like Lying*, and *You Complete Me*, a profound exploration of cultivating a godly marriage, co-authored with his wife, Wanda L. Brandon.

A beloved pastor, teacher, mentor, and father, Bishop Brandon is deeply committed to his family and community. He is the proud father of five children: Queenesia, Jasmine, Isaiah, Elijah, and the late Larry III. His prayer for every individual he encounters is that they be blessed, challenged, inspired, and transformed. His guiding motto is simple yet powerful: "We are better together."

Another Book by this Author

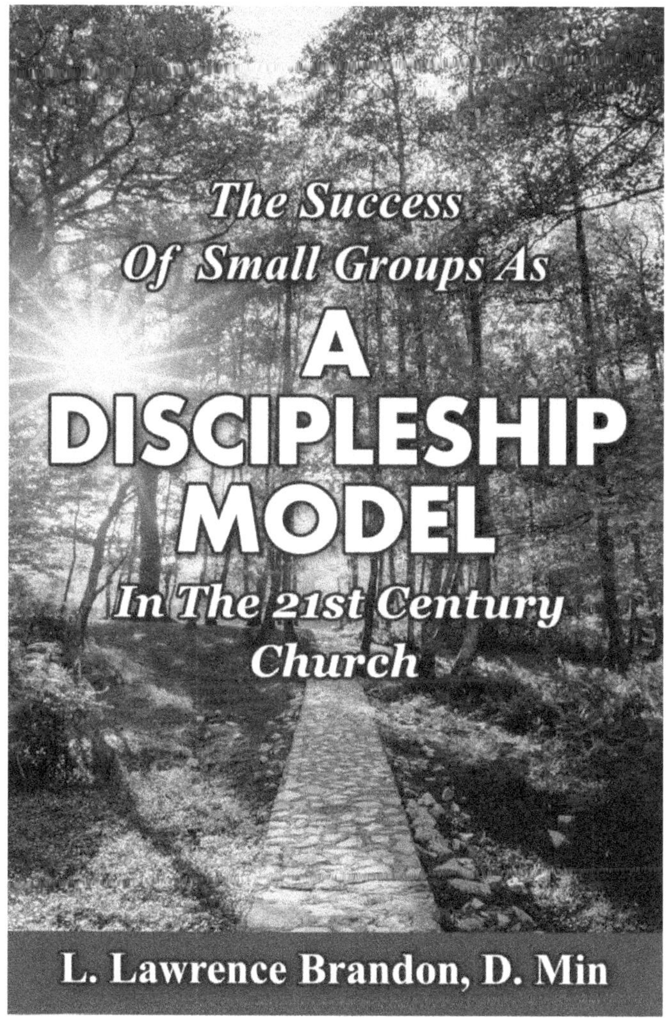

www.ingramcontent.com/pod-product-compliance
Lightning Source LLC
LaVergne TN
LVHW010918110826
845149LV00013B/2416

* 9 7 8 1 9 6 7 2 8 2 9 5 1 *